LiCK

puppies

PHOTOGRAPHS BY TY FOSTER

KNOCK
KNOCK.
VENICE, CALIFORNIA

Published by Knock Knock LLC
1635-B Electric Ave.
Venice, CA 90291
knockknockstuff.com
Knock Knock is a registered trademark of Knock Knock LLC

Photographs by Ty Foster
www.tyfoster.com

Special thanks to: Companion Pet Rescue
(www.cprdogs.com), Puppy Love, and
Lauren Meren of Puppies of Westport.

ISBN: 978-160106853-8
UPC: 825703-50229-9

10 9 8 7 6 5 4 3 2

To V. There's an elephant in the room.

LiCK puppies. No one ever had a bad day taking pictures of puppies. That's because, as a wise comic strip character once observed, happiness really is a warm puppy. Literally. With this book, you are basically holding pure happiness in the palms of your hands.

LICK Puppies represents many hours of "toil" behind the camera as I gave these furry balls of love their very first taste of peanut butter—then photographed the *aww*-inspiring results. I feel certain that each page will crush you with its crippling, majestic puppy cuteness. (Sorry, but just imagine what it was like for me.)

Working with puppies is like eating a bag of fun-sized candy bars: each one is absolutely delicious, and you can't wait to unwrap the next, and the next. I hope you feel the same as you flip through these pages. Please devour these babies with gusto (like a puppy eating peanut butter!), and return to them as often as needed for an infusion of pure, delicious, fuzzy, warm puppy love.

—Ty Foster

Joey
(Goldendoodle)

Romeo
(Dachshund)

Ollie
(Puggle)

Moose
(German Shepherd)

Sheba
(Boglen Terrier)

Penelope
(Goldendoodle)

Buttons
(Shih Tzu /
Yorkshire Terrier)

Hudson
(Labrador Retriever)

Oscar
(Havanese)

Daisy
(English Bulldog)

Rudy
(Sharpei / Bulldog)

Pat (Yorkiepoo),
Sam (Clumber
Spaniel)

Sparky (Chihuahua),
Stan (English
Bulldog)

Ramona
(Shepherd Mix)

Clifford
(Chihuahua)

Roxie
(Yorkshire Terrier /
Bichon Frise)

Chelsea
(Toy Australian
Shepherd)

Charlie
(Pekapoo)

Luke
(Cavalier King
Charles Spaniel /
Schnauzer)

Lola
(Chesapeake Bay
Retriever Mix)

Gracie
(Boston Terrier Mix)

J. R.
(Rottweiler)

Freckles
(Blue Heeler)

Sparky
(Chihuahua)

Lulu
(Mini English
Bulldog)

Casey
(Silkypoo)

Bear
(Soft-Coated
Wheaten Terrier)

Mathilda
(Bulldog / Boxer)

Gizmo
(French Bulldog /
Boston Terrier)

Popcorn, Peanuts
(Palaneses)

Ollie
(Puggle)

Pancakes
(Boston Terrier)

Arrow
(Beagle / Bulldog)

Penelope (Gold-
endoodle), **Toto**
(Yorkshire Terrier)

Toto
(Yorkshire Terrier)

Casper
(Beagle Mix)

Elsa
(Mastiff)

Morrisey
(Jack Russell Terrier /
German Shepherd)

Sugar
(Lab Mix)

Goldie
(Cocker Spaniel)

Bandit (Maltese / Yorkshire Terrier), **Charlie** (Pekapoo)

Olive (Cavalier King Charles Spaniel / Poodle)

Roberta (Shih Tzu / Maltese)

Sugar (Lab Mix)

Hunter (Lab Mix)

Stan (English Bulldog), **Pancakes** (Boston Terrier)

Stan (English Bulldog)

Olive (Cavalier King Charles Spaniel / Poodle)

Pepper (Australian Cattle Dog / Shepherd)

Rosie, Teddy (Yorkshire Terriers)

Butter (Beagle / Bulldog), **Sheba** (Boglen Terrier), **Beans** (Beagle / Bulldog)

Missy (Cocker Spaniel)

Betty (Sharpei / Beagle)

Sheba (Boglen Terrier)

Mick, Paco (Shiba Inus)

Abby, Honey (Labrador Retriever / Shetland Sheepdogs)

Sparky (Chihuahua)

Maximus (Bichon Frise / Poodle)

Zelda (French Bulldog)

Marty (Chihuahua / Dachshund)

Doof
(French Bulldog /
Rat Terrier)

Sam
(Clumber Spaniel)

Katie
(Pomeranian)

Viola
(Australian
Shepherd Dog Mix)

Sunny
(Pomeranian)

Shane
(Mini Labradoodle)

Abby
(Labrador Retriever /
Shetland Sheepdog)

Rusty
(Puggle)

Moose
(German Shepherd)

Waffles
(Dachshund)

Bruno
(English Bulldog)

Spud
(Aussiepoo)

Casey
(Silkypoo)

Romeo, Kelly
(Dachshunds)

Gus
(Tibetan Terrier)

Lady
(Cocker Spaniel)

Joey
(Goldendoodle)

Ramona (Shepherd
Mix), **Casper** (Beagle
Mix)

Gracie
(Boston Terrier Mix)

Freckles (Blue
Heeler), **Rudy**
(Sharpei / Bulldog)